HEART
of the
HIMALAYA

DAVID PATERSON
PEAK PUBLISHING LTD
JAICO PUBLISHING HOUSE

© Peak Publishing Ltd., 1997
© Text and photographs, David Paterson, 1997
None of the photographs in this book have been electronically enhanced.
Some of the photographs have previously appeared in
'Nepal - The Mountains of Heaven' (H. Hamilton 1990).

First published in Great Britain by:
Peak Publishing Ltd.,
88 Cavendish Road,
London SW12 0DF.

Exclusively distributed in India, Nepal, Pakistan,
Bangladesh and Sri Lanka by:
Jaico Publishing House,
Mumbai, Delhi, Bangalore,
Calcutta, Hyderabad, Chennai.

ISBN 0 9521908 2 6

British Library cataloguing in publication data applied for.

Paterson, David
Heart of the Himalaya
1. The Himalayas
2. Nepal
3. Photography

Designed by Peak Publishing
Typeset in Bookman 12/16
Printed in Hong Kong by C&C Offset Printing Co., Ltd.

Contents

Early morning at Bodnath, Kathmandu

The Annapurna range, from the Thulobugin Ridge

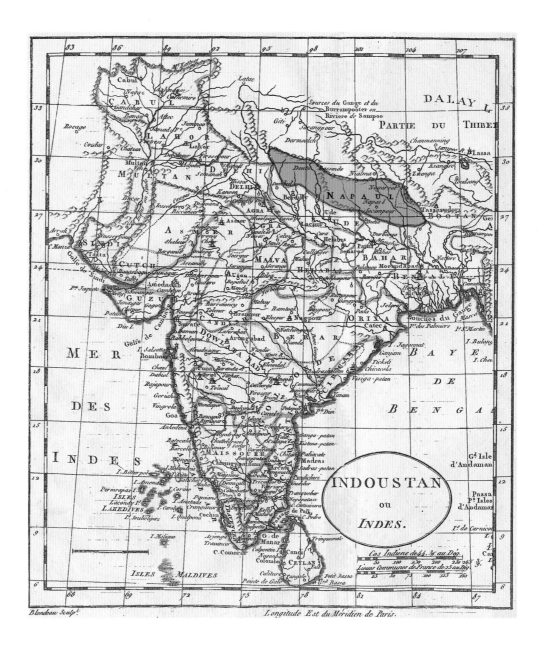

PREFACE

The small country of Nepal - five hundred miles of longtitude by a hundred of latitude - lies on the main Himalayan chain, squeezed between much larger neighbours, Tibet and India, north and south. Apart from a narrow strip of lowland - the terai - which merges into the vast Gangetic plains of northern India, the landscape of Nepal is wholly mountainous. Rising from the terai, the gentle hills of the Siwalik range are much the lowest barrier a traveller would meet on a journey north through the country. Next come the Lesser Himalaya - much bigger and wilder hills rising occasionally as high as fifteen thousand feet, their steep limestone slopes deeply scarred by monsoon-fed streams. In most other countries of the world, these mountains would be thought remarkable; here, they go almost unnoticed. Towering behind them, the snow- and ice-clad summits of the Greater Himalaya reduce all else to insignificance. Ranging from around eighteen thousand to over twenty-nine thousand feet (5500 to 8800m) in height, the greatest mountain range in the world sweeps in a vast crescent more than fifteen hundred miles long, from the borders of Burma in the east to northern Afghanistan in the extreme west, with Nepal close to its geographic centre. No other country can rival her concentration of high peaks. In the whole world, only fourteen mountains rise above twenty-six thousand feet (8000m), and eight of these are in Nepal. She of course has the highest of all, Mount Everest - Chomolungma - as well as the third, fourth, fifth, sixth, seventh, eighth and fourteenth highest. In addition to these giants, she has almost one hundred peaks of more than twenty-three thousand feet (7000m).

You run out of superlatives trying to describe Nepal - the highest mountains, deepest gorges and fastest rivers - it is a country of mythic qualities, where visitors flock to climb and trek among the mountains, and it is difficult to exaggerate Nepal's attractions. Nowhere else has the amazing range of terrain, or the speed of transition from sub-tropical to high-alpine in such a brief passage of time or space. You stroll along a valley among fields of tobacco, rice or sugar-cane, or sit in a village shaded by hibiscus and frangipani, but only have to lift your gaze to where glaciers tumble from the frigid summits of some of the highest peaks on earth. On a first visit, impressions can be overwhelming. Strolling through a sylvan landscape with undertones of 15th- or 16th-century Europe, few can resist being drawn into the feeling that they have wandered into an enchanted land where time has stood still; and in a way they have.

But there is another side to Nepal. This is a country whose average income, literacy level, and life-expectancy are among the lowest in the world, and whose rates of infant mortality, child-labour and -prostitution are distressingly high. All this results from Nepal being one of the poorest countries on earth, with very little manufacturing industry, almost no exploitable mineral resources, and barely enough good agricultural land to feed her burgeoning native population (as well as tens of thousands of Tibetan refugees and the constant influx of migrants across the long uncontrolled border with India). With help from China, a hydro-electric industry is being developed which may lead to significant exports of energy; but for now tourism is almost the sole provider of hard currency for the thousand and one imports which, at the end of the 20th century, it seems no country can live without.

I have been travelling to Nepal for the better part of twenty years, and in that time there have been many changes. During a recent visit I stopped at a police post to read some vital statistics on trekkers passing through Jomosom, the main administrative centre for Mustang in the west of the country. In 1995, the last full year for which they had complete figures, some seventeen-and-a-half thousand foreigners passed through that one check-point - as many as trekked in all of Nepal during 1979, the year of my own first visit. Admittedly, Jomosom sits on a very popular trail, but here is evidence that in some areas trekking is changing from minority recreation to mass tourism, with all that implies. Worries have frequently been expressed about the environmental damage caused by large volume trekking, including de-forestation along the busier routes. It has been calculated that a foreign trekker uses, directly or indirectly, twenty times as much firewood per day as a native Nepali - hot water for washing, shaving, showering, laundry, and an apparent need for complicated hot meals three times a day and roaring camp-fires in the evenings. The Nepali authorities have moved to control a lot of the tree-felling, however, and in all National Parks there is now strict monitoring of fuel sources.

Of course, tourists do bring benefits, not least the income which local people can earn by providing services, and there has been some raising of consciousness, too. The learning process is a two-way thing, however, and visitors here have much to learn from the country people of Nepal and their gentle, tolerant way of life. Nevertheless, it is certainly true that increased awareness of matters such as education, health and environmental care has come in part from contact with trekking groups and climbing expeditions.

Other changes are making their presence felt, too. Whereas even ten years or so ago there were few motorable roads in Nepal, today new roads in many areas are bringing increased mobility to a population which was, until quite recently, restricted to travel on foot. Soon after the roads come electrical power-lines, some of which are not sited all that sympathetically, bearing in mind the landscapes they pass through. Still, their arrival must be counted a blessing by the people of the countryside, who suffer almost twelve hours of darkness every night of the year, and now, as well as electric light, may even have access to a telephone.

Of course, for visitors, especially those with some experience of Nepal, there is bound to be disappointment at seeing trucks and buses grinding up previously unspoilt valleys, and lines of pylons traversing glorious landscapes or bisecting the main streets of priceless medieval villages; perhaps by the time these power-lines are due for renewal, awareness will have been raised another few notches, and their replacements will be more sensitively situated. The buses may sometimes transport almost as many trekkers as locals, and the trucks are often full of beer, Coke and Fanta which the trekking-lodges will sell, but they also carry construction materials, people and goods to and from market, children to school, and students to college. We in the west have enjoyed to the full the benefits of modern transport, communications and technology; it would be mean-spirited in the extreme (and futile) to attempt to deny them to the Nepalese. What is shocking, perhaps, is to witness a village or a region making a forced leap from the sixteenth century direct to the present time; or to see - as I did in a remote village in the Ganesh Himal area in 1986 - people whose own culture did not even include the wheel, watching an Indian 'Dallas' on television. (The TV set and video-recorder were run from a small petrol-driven generator; all had been carried to the village on mens' backs, and the people were paying a local enterpreneur, in whose house it was set up, a few rupees per hour to watch.) Most environmental damage is reversible given time, but the problems likely to be caused by this kind of cultural mayhem could be far more serious and long-lasting.

An unstoppable process is under way in much of the Nepalese countryside, and who can tell where it will lead? Though the people have survived down the centuries, living and working in their traditional ways, life can be hard. Now, as the 20th century creeps ever further out from the towns, they begin to have an inkling of the easy life of the West, and they want that; they see the expensive possessions of the trekkers who pass through their villages - and they want those. Who can blame them? Change is rushing down upon them, and how can they be helped, or persuaded, to hold on to values which are disappearing fast elsewhere - things like simple dignity, self-reliance, and the closeness of family and village life? Away from the trucks and TV sets the hill people of Nepal still exist, at best, in a state of innocence which is wonderful to see, and it is reassuring that here and there whole districts do not want roads or trekking-routes to come through their land; there still are people who value the traditional way of life. But they are like Canute and the waves; if the 20th century has made inroads, the 21st will be irresistible. Of course, trekkers and climbers are not the whole problem - but they are part of the problem and should be aware of that. There are all sorts of ways we can minimise our impact on the environment and peoples of the hills.

 I was lucky enough to have first visited Nepal when most trails were still quiet and the local people had a warm welcome for everyone who passed their doors. Those were golden years for me, and even after all this time Nepal still works her magic well enough for there to be a few distant corners I might still hope to reach, before the roads and the buses do.

Rice fields in the Arun valley, East Nepal

Tumlingtar, in the early morning

Rice-fields near Birethanti, West Nepal

Immature dragonfly, Kathmandu valley

Woman and child in barleyfield, Helambu

Dawn light on foothills near Pokhara

Porter near Amjilassa, Kangchenjunga region

Peak 7 and prayer flags, Barun Valley, East Nepal

Sunrise at Bijeswari, Kathmandu

The Kathmandu valley

We were moving athwart the grain of the land - down into deep valleys, across foaming torrents or broader, swift-flowing rivers, and up the far hillsides.

- Sir John Hunt 'The Ascent of Everest'

Close at hand, and throwing their cold shadows over us, two mighty peaks, the nearer pyramidal in form, the further double-headed, rose in tiers of unmitigated precipices.

- Douglas Freshfield 'Round Kangchenjunga'

Dawn ridges at Gul Bhanjyang, Helambu

A SHORT HISTORY

Climbers and explorers cast longing looks at Nepal and her unrivalled wealth of high mountains for many decades before they were permitted to begin the process of exploration. This was forbidden territory, as Nepal followed a course of careful neutrality between her giant neighbours; a policy which meant the exclusion of all foreigners. The beginnings of mountaineering as a sport - a European invention of the 19th century - coincided with 'The Great Game' when the continental powers, principally India and Russia (and to a lesser extent China) competed with each other for influence and control over the vast territories of central Asia, and their trade and natural resources. India at that time meant, of course, the British Raj, and many of the soldiers and bureaucrats sent to police or administer its northern territories were instinctive explorers whose curiosity was aroused by the unknown ranges, tantalisingly close, just across the border.

It followed that the earliest forays into Nepal came from Sikkim, with which it shares a long and mountainous frontier. It was relatively easy for small parties to slip across the border, and from the late 1840's onwards the northeast corner of Nepal saw a succession of intruders from British-administered territory, eager to survey, botanise or generally explore this fascinating swathe of country. Many of these were given the nod by British officialdom, and some, notably the Pundits (native Indian surveyors, trained by the Survey of India) were on the official but clandestine business of surveying the closed lands of Nepal and Tibet. Kangchenjunga, whose summit lies on the Sikkimese border, was spectacularly visible from Darjeeling, less than fifty miles away, and the mountain and its satellite peaks soon became targets. The first real mountaineer to appear was W.W. Graham, well known for his Scottish and Alpine exploits, who climbed several peaks in the Kabru range just south of Kangchenjunga, and claimed to have reached the summit of Kabru itself, in 1883. (Since Kabru is a giant of twenty-four thousand feet (7320m) this would have been a sensational ascent; most opinion has been that Graham was simply mistaken about the identity of the mountain he had climbed.) In 1899, another well-known British climber of the day appeared on the Himalayan scene - Douglas Freshfield. His aim was to complete a circuit of the whole Kangchenjunga massif, and in this he was almost entirely successful. His long circum-navigation included, inevitably, an illegal incursion into Nepal (and brushes with minor officials) and he was the first European with a mountaineer's vision to examine the north-western aspects of the peak. His impressions, published in 1903 in his classic book Round Kangchenjunga, were to influence attempts on the mountain for the next fifty years.

The great Himalayan pioneer, Dr A.M. Kellas, was next on the scene, climbing and exploring intensively along the Nepal-Sikkim border in the early years of the century, but the first attempt on Kangchenjunga itself was made by an ill-fated group led by the 'diabolist' Aleister Crowley in 1905. They reached some twenty-one thousand feet (6400m) on the south face, climbing from the Yalung Valley in Nepal, but the expedition is notable mainly for having recorded the first deaths on the mountain. No further visits were made to the mountain until 1921, when another celebrated British climber, Raeburn, made a light-weight attempt from the Yalung Valley. Three other serious attempts were made on Kangchenjunga during the years 1929 to 1931 - two strong German expeditions led by the formidable Dr Paul Bauer, and a large international group which included the leading British climber, Frank Smythe, led by the Swiss, Professor G. Dyrenfurth. Of these,

the German attempts were on the east flank of the mountain, from Sikkim, and startled the climbing world by reaching over twenty-four and twenty-five thousand feet (7320 and 7620m) respectively; but the Dyrenfurth group was to be the first to ask for, and be granted, official permission from the government of Nepal to enter and climb on their territory. They crossed the Kang La from Sikkim and descended into the Yalung Valley, before making their way to Ghunsa on the west side of the range. From there they continued to Pang Pema below the north face of Kangchen-junga. Though their assault on the mountain was unsuccessful, one barrier at least had been breached by their presence, with official sanction, on Nepalese soil, and they did climb several other peaks in the region.

In the years up to the second World War, the other Nepalese peak to receive a great deal of attention was, of course, Mount Everest. The Nepalese never allowed these expeditions to cross their land, however, and all seven pre-war British parties approached the mountain from Tibet. (Two old Kangchenjunga pioneers, Kellas and Raeburn, were brought together on the first Everest expedition of 1921. Kellas, sadly, died from dysentery and exhaustion during the walk through Tibet, and ill-health forced Raeburn's resignation as climbing leader.) The achievements and ultimate failure of all these pre-war expeditions are, of course, extensively documented and their history, and that of the many instances of outstanding individual effort, selflessness and bravery, is well known. The names of Mallory and Irvine have virtually entered the English language as a synonym for gallant failure, and for anyone who has stood on the most minor of Himalayan peaks, the realisation of how tough all these men were, in their Shetland sweaters and Norfolk tweed jackets, is shocking. Following the first reconnaissance in 1921, the next year saw Bruce and Finch reach over twenty-seven thousand feet (8300m); in the fateful year of 1924, Mallory and Irvine died somewhere above twenty-seven thousand, seven hundred feet (8450m), Norton reached over twenty-eight thousand feet (8540m) without supplementary oxygen, and a fourth team member, Odell, lived continuously above twenty-three thousand feet (7000m) for two weeks. Similar heights were reached on several of the other expeditions.

In the years immediately before the war, three names would appear on the rosters of these British efforts which would resound through later Himalayan annals - Eric Shipton and Bill Tilman, for their unequalled record of exploration - and Sherpa Tenzing, of Everest fame. At much the same time, a small private expedition to the Yalung valley, to the south-east of Kangchenjunga, included someone else who was to play a crucial role in future events on Everest - John (later Sir John) Hunt.

The war years caused a hiatus in Himalayan mountaineering, but in the late 1940's political developments within Nepal and the invasion of Tibet by China were to cause a sudden and radical change in access to the mountains. Tibet, which had been open at least to large officially-sponsored expeditions, was abruptly and completely closed, and Nepal, which had previously refused all approaches but one, began to give quiet encouragement. In 1950, an Anglo-American reconnaissance which included the irrepressible Bill Tilman, was made to the Khumbu (Everest) region, and in 1951 an Anglo-New Zealand recce to the same area was led by Eric Shipton and included the name Edmund Hillary. Events seemed to be leading to a climax on Everest, with the right people coming together at the right time in a seemingly inexorable process, but the strand of amateurishness which had run through pre-war British mountaineering was to make a fateful reappearance. When permission was sought for pre- and post-monsoon attempts on Everest in 1952, to their chagrin the Brits discovered they had left things too late - it had already been granted to the Swiss.

The Sharphu range, Kangchenjunga region

Peak 7 from Mera, Makalu region

The news created uproar within the British mountaineering establishment; however, panic measures failed to secure them a place on the Swiss expeditions. There was good reason for the British to fear they might lose the prize they had struggled for since 1921. Not only had the Swiss assembled a crack team of mainly professional alpinists, but already in 1950, a French expedition similarly composed of alpine guides, led by Maurice Herzog, had stunned the climbing world by pioneering a route to the foot of Annapurna, in unknown west Nepal, and climbing it at the first attempt. Annapurna was then the highest mountain in the world to have been climbed, and the first over twenty-six thousand feet (8000m).

The Swiss team very nearly climbed Everest in 1952, but not quite, reaching a height of over twenty-eight thousand feet (8600m), and only their lack of experience of climbing at such extreme altitudes, and bad weather, prevented them from reaching the summit. In the same year the British were allowed the consolation of an attempt on a different Nepalese giant - Cho Oyu, another peak over twenty-six thousand feet (8000m), less than twenty miles to the west of Everest. The expedition leader again was Eric Shipton, who had become almost an automatic choice for the position, but they failed to make any serious impression on the mountain. Before turning for home the climbers split up into smaller groups to pursue individual goals, climbing and exploring in many parts of the region, and achieved superb results. However, the question began to be asked - was Shipton after all the right man to lead another large-scale campaign, such as the next Everest expedition would have to be? In the to-and-fro which followed within the ranks of the British climbing establishment, it was John Hunt's name which emerged as the next leader, and the rest, as they say, is history.

Hunt's determined leadership plus a stronger and more professional team, the best available equipment and perhaps above all the utter determination of the summit pair, Hillary and Tenzing, combined to give the British, at last, the success on Everest which had eluded them for so long. (Though, of course, no Briton actually reached the summit. The first British climbers to reach the top of Everest were Doug Scott and Dougal Haston, in 1975.) If, in the years before the war, many nations - notably the British, French, Germans and Americans - had failed repeatedly in their attempts to climb any of the fourteen Himalayan giants over twenty-six thousand feet (8000m), now they were all to be climbed within the space of a few years. With Annapurna in 1950 and Everest in 1953, a major psychological barrier had been overcome; equipment and protective clothing were improving by leaps and bounds, and a new generation of climbers - more skilful if not tougher than their predecessors, and certainly more willing to press things to a conclusion - was coming on to the scene. Nepal's six other 8000m peaks fell in quick succession - Cho Oyu next in 1954, Makalu and Kangchenjunga in 1955, Lhotse and Manaslu in 1956, and Dhaulagiri, perhaps the hardest, in 1960. The nationalities involved were British, French, Swiss, Austrian and Japanese, and Nepalese nationals - Sherpas - had been in the summit parties on three occasions. The first great era of Himalayan climbing was drawing to a close, as one by one all the highest peaks were climbed; first all those over 8000m, then the most attractive or accessible over 7000m.

For obvious reasons, all the 8000m peaks were initially climbed by what mountaineers believed to be the easiest routes, involving the least amount of technical climbing. Early in its development Himalayan mountaineering had evolved its own method, in which a large team of climbers, supported by many more Sherpas and porters, would lay seige to their peak. A line of fixed camps would slowly reach up the mountain, abandoned in heavy storms, re-established and re-occupied when the weather improved, until the highest camp was near enough the summit for an attempt to be made, and if the expedition had sufficient resources, several summit bids could be made from the top camp. All along, however, there had been exponents of smaller, lighter expeditions which could climb the mountain much more quickly, taking advantage of any short spell of fine weather; and much more economically, too. A major disadvantage of the seige style was its expense, resulting from the large numbers of people and huge quantities of supplies and equipment. In alpine style, a small group of climbers - often close friends - with or without Sherpa support, would move continuously up the mountain, carrying their equipment and tents with them, laying up during poor spells and continuing as soon as better weather permitted. Much of the exploratory climbing around Kangchenjunga was done (by Raeburn, Kellas and others) in this fashion, and as early as 1895 a group of only three British climbers, including the celebrated alpinist Albert (A.F.) Mummery, travelled to India to climb Nanga Parbat, a peak of twenty-six thousand, six hundred feet (8125m). Mummery and two of his Ghurkha porters disappeared during the expedition and were presumed to have been killed in an avalanche, but the boldness of their endeavour was greatly admired.

It was an early prototype for the lightweight

style of climbing which started to appear in Nepal and elsewhere during the late 1960's. Instead of grinding up the easiest way, small groups of highly-skilled climbers now began to look to the giant faces of these peaks to provide superb technical climbing. Some routes were still big and intimidating enough to require an amalgam of seige and alpine styles, and the British mountaineer, Chris Bonington, was an adept organiser and leader of this type of expedition. The south face of Annapurna, and the south-west face of Everest both fell to this approach; Bonington himself, often with the Nottingham climber Doug Scott, made several assaults on smaller, very challenging peaks. Scott became one of the leading exponents of lightweight climbs on large mountains, and in Nepal he climbed Nuptse, Chamlang, Makalu and Kangchenjunga.

Another development which ran in parallel with the growth of alpine-style climbing was the gradual abandonment of artificial (bottled) oxygen. From the early days when it had been seen as vital for survival on the largest peaks, the use of bottled oxygen had gradually come to be regarded as unethical, except perhaps in emergencies. Scott and others had showed that big peaks could be successfully climbed without it, and in 1978 Reinhold Messner and Peter Habeler, while attached to a much larger Austrian expedition, reached the summit of Everest without oxygen. (Messner was to go on to make similar, oxygen-less ascents of all fourteen 8000m peaks.)

During the 1980's and 90's the number of new ascents and new routes has multiplied rapidly. Nations still queue to put their teams on the summit of Everest by the traditional South Col route, and the giant peaks will always attract expeditions, but the trend has continued away from large expeditions. Small groups of friends look for new and harder routes on the biggest peaks; they climb in winter; and of course they climb without oxygen. It might be thought that by now mountaineers might have exhausted all the interesting possibilities, but that is far from being the case. Nepal has scores of peaks over 7000m - many still unclimbed - and it is unlikely that anyone even knows how many there are over 6000m (and 6100m is twenty thousand feet). Many of these have never been named, let alone explored or climbed, and every mountain has several faces and ridges, all of which invite exploration. Even when every summit has been reached - a distant possibility - there will still be an infinity of new climbs waiting to be done, and climbers will always be able to find their own challenges in the mountains. The history of climbing in the Nepal Himalaya still lies mainly in the future.

Nuptse in evening light, from Lobuche

Sunset on Lhotse, Everest range

The Everest group from Gokyo Peak

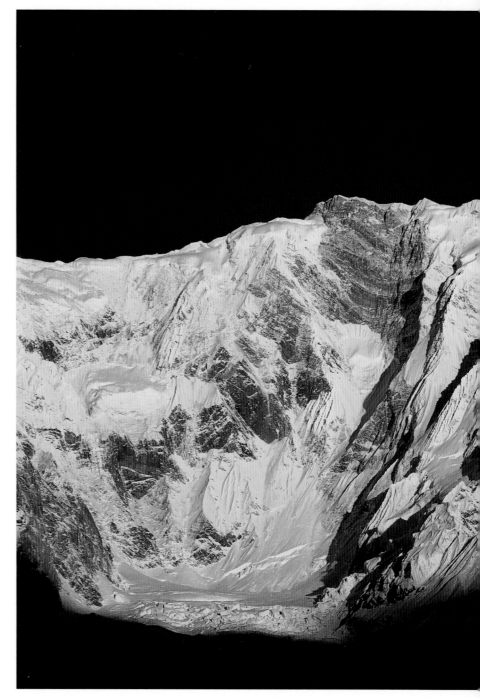

First sun on Annapurna South Face

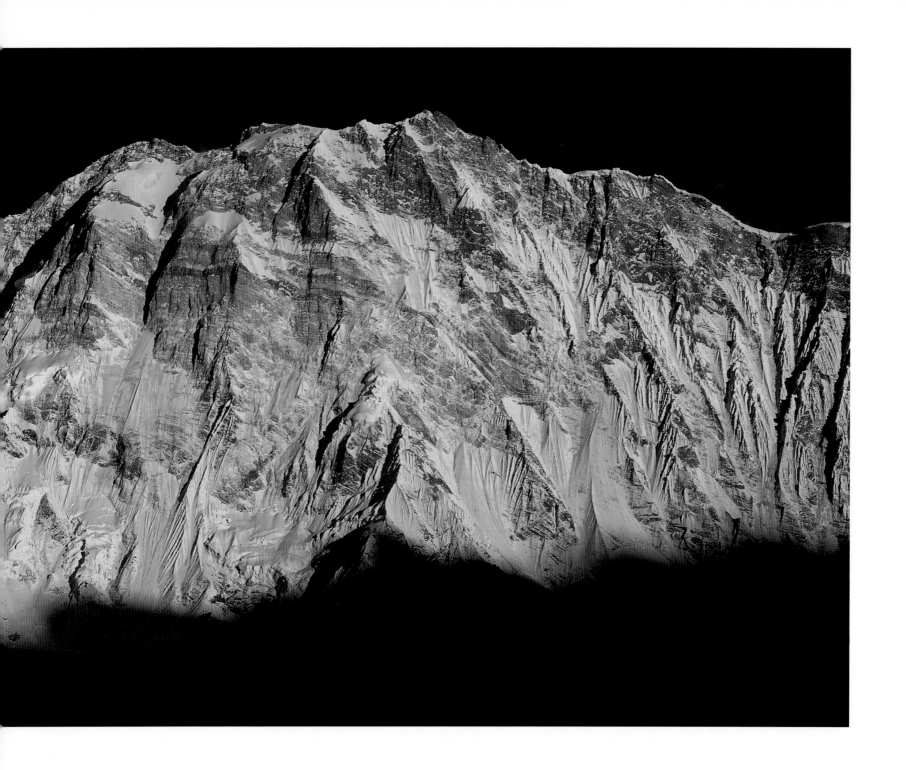

Kangchenjunga from Pangpema

Makalu, from Shers[o]

Tilicho Peak, Manang

Sunset over the Pangsung ridge, Langtang

Porter in the Barun Valley

Naya Kanga, Langtang region

Kang Nachugo, Rolwaling region

Machhapuchare, the Fish-Tail, from the Annapurna Sanctuary

Gokyo Ri

Ama Dablam from Lobuche Base Camp, Everest region

Choughs over Kongde Ri, Khumbu

The upper Everest valley, from Lobuche Peak

Chamlang from Sherson, Makalu region

I walked through mists and clouds, breathing the thin air of high altitude, and stepping on ice and snow, till at last through a gateway of clouds, as it seemed to the very paths of the sun and moon, I reached the summit.

– Basho 'The Narrow Road to Deep North'

Rock, and snow peaks all around, the sky, and great birds and black rivers - what words are there to seize such ringing splendour?

– Peter Matthiessen 'The Snow Leopard'

Dawn over the foothills, Helambu

Passes & Failures

Because weeks of planning have gone into the preparation for a long trek, this does not always mean that traversing a seventeen- or eighteen-thousand-foot pass, which can look so insignificant on a map, is going to be a pushover. Many people underestimate the difficulties of these crossings, and I have been the victim of my own optimism in this respect more than once. When bad weather strikes, it is rarely the expedition members, wrapped in goretex and down jackets, and with expensive mountain boots, who really suffer. It is the porters, usually much more lightly equipped (and less well nourished) who are at some risk, and it is rare for a season to pass without at least one fatality among their ranks; cases of frost-bite are commonplace. Sometimes snow conditions can be just too deep and dangerous to take porters into, and if this kind of decision has to be made, it is never worth risking other lives just to finish a trek, even if it means that part of a cherished plan has to be abandoned.

The message is, I suppose, that Himalayan passes are higher than alpine summits in most other parts of the world, and shouldn't be trifled with; this is mountaineering, and as a Japanese climbing friend of mine once said, the important part of mountaineering is survival - for everyone in the party.

The longest, highest pass I've been fortunate to cross was the Tesi Lapcha, which connects the remote valley of Rolwaling with the Sherpa region of Khumbu, to the south of Everest. From the last inhabited village in Rolwaling to the first in Khumbu was four days' walking, more than half of the time on glaciers, and the high point of the pass was just under nineteen thousand feet (5800m). It was hard work, but real adventure, and the feeling of remoteness - of really being out there - was superb. The second day after leaving Beding, in Rolwaling, the weather was poor - low overcast with a biting wind and flurries of snow - and we were all a little apprehensive, but the third day was fine and we hurried to get up and over the summit of the pass before nightfall. Another day later we were safely in Thame, in Khumbu. We had encountered no real problems, but only two days later a French party going the other way was torn apart by ferocious winds - equipment scattered and porters blown away, literally. I had no idea then whether they were foolhardy or simply unlucky, but it showed just how fine was the margin for error.

Some years later, with a photographer friend, Mike McQueen, I crossed another remote pass, almost as long and hard as the Tesi Lapcha. This was the Lapsang La, in the Kangchenjunga region, away in the farthest corner of east Nepal. The party was nine in number - Mike and I, two Sherpas and five porters. Speed of movement once at altitude is a key to success on high passes, but this can only be achieved by allowing time for acclimatisation. On this long trek we had already climbed to eighteen thousand feet above Kangchenjunga north base-camp at Pang Pema, and had spent some ten or twelve days above ten thousand feet before reaching the foot of the pass, so in that sense at least we were well prepared.

The Lapsang La leads from the Sherpa village of Ghunsa, two to three days' walk south of Pang Pema, through the southern tail of the Kangchenjunga range to the Yalung valley, and the only member of the party who had any knowledge of the route was one of our porters, Dawa, who claimed to have carried there for a trekking group some years before. It is hard to find a reliable figure for the height of the pass, and on the day our altimeter showed over nineteen thousand feet (5800m), which tends to confirm the figure shown on trekking maps. However, the true height is probably nearer eighteen thousand. The trail from Ghunsa, rarely trekked, is used by the local people to get up to high yak pastures in summer, or to cross over to Yalung on the east side of the range, en route to trade in Sikkim, in northern India. On the first day it climbs steeply for two or three hours through fine mixed forest. Still trending upwards, it skirts the snout of the Yamatari Glacier, crosses a couple of vigourous streams, and meanders over two craggy ridges - ancient moraines - eventually reaching a large stony plateau. The day was clear, cold and sunny, and as we gained height there were fine views back across the Ghunsa valley to the Sharphu range. There were no problems until we came to the second stream, which was deep and fast-flowing. We chose to cross where it divided into three smaller channels, and the first two went easily but the third was white water at least crotch-deep, and we searched up and down the near bank for a good way across. Eventually a sapling was cut down, the trunk stripped of its branches, and we filed out into the torrent, clutching the bare pole for mutual support. On the far bank a fire was lit, and we lay around a while to rest and dry out. Three hours later, just before dusk, we reached the yak pasture at around sixteen thousand feet (4880m) where in the distance eight or nine of the beasts were calmly grazing, and set up our tents in the lee of several large boulders.

In the morning we were up early and walking soon after five am, in pitch dark and freezing temperatures. Our route now took us across the yak pasture and another stream to the foot of a large moraine about five hundred feet high. The steep rocks leading to the top of this were covered with verglas - thin, hard ice smeared like treacle over every surface - and a sprinkling of powder snow. We crept carefully upwards, most of us following a shallow gully which offered some feelings of security; Nima, who had opted to stay on the crest of the rocks, slipped and took a fifteen-foot fall; luckily for all of us he escaped with bruising. High above, early sunshine was creeping across the south face of Jannu, savagely steep and seamed with ice, and as we crested the rocks we came up into full daylight ourselves for the first time.

The way ahead was easier now, along a lateral moraine and eventually down on to the rubble-covered glacier descending southwest from Boktoh, the twenty-thousand-foot peak which stands immediately to the north of the pass. Everest, Lhotse and Makalu were just visible, far on the western horizon, though within minutes distant cloud bubbled up to obscure the view. In the early morning we had suffered from cold; now it became punishingly hot as we toiled up the glacier into a wide basin surrounded on three sides by steep cliffs and ice-falls. The landscape was unspectacular and bleak, grey rubble covered nine-tenths of the glacier, and there was no hint of vegetation to soften our surroundings under the glare of a mid-day sun. The only mountain in close view was Boktoh, and, disconcertingly, there was no sign anywhere of the pass. Fins of blue ice rose through the debris of the glacier and minor avalanches rattled down nearby as we scanned the apparently continuous line of crags; but there had to be a way, and I set off to scout ahead. Above the dry glacier we had been on all morning, recent snow lay thickly on the rocks, and moving up towards the foot of the cliffs, almost at once I came on a line of footprints. They were a few days old, and had melted and re-frozen a few times, but it was clear that two people - probably locals - had come through here, heading downhill. We had only to retrace their steps to find the pass. I shouted for the others to come on.

An hour later we turned a sharp corner of the cliffs to find a snow-slope about forty-five degrees steep and a hundred and fifty feet high leading up to a gap; above the snowy crest only blue sky was visible; I kicked and chopped steps in the hard snow and in five minutes reached the top, breathless. The col was a metre wide and ten long, just big enough for all of us and our loads to perch on.

Un-named peaks in south Rolwaling

Drolambo Glacier, and peaks on the Tibetan border, Tesi Lapcha pass

The enormous cliffs of Boktoh soared above us on the left, and to the right a ridge ran up to a series of minor peaks, their rock summits clear of snow but with large glaciers descending into the basin we had recently left. Ahead, a steep slope several kilometres long led down into the dark gulf of the Yalung Valley. The way ahead was through a scary-looking jumble of rocks of every size from a football to a house, with no visible trail anywhere; but at least the slope, facing south-east, was largely clear of snow. Across the valley, a single snow-peak was framed by the walls of the glacial trench into which we were about to descend.

At dusk we stumbled from the rocks onto a sandy beach beside a stream of clear water, with the giant snow-dome of Kabru and her satellite peaks glimmering in the fading light across the Yalung Valley. There were still more slopes ahead to descend, but it was too late, too dark, and we had already been going nearly fifteen hours and were exhausted. Somehow, the tents were pitched on the little beach, we drank tea and fell inside. In the morning the sun shone on a grassy ramp leading easily down into the Yalung; we were past all the difficulties and had crossed the Lapsang La.

At other times, success did not come so readily, or at all. In 1984, as part of a much longer trek, I had wanted to take the high trail around Dhaulagiri from the Kali Gandaki valley in west Nepal, but was prevented by prolonged snowfall. Coming back to try again twelve years later, I never dreamed that fate would deal me the same hand.

On that first visit to the area I was trekking with an old friend, John Beatty, with whom I had crossed the Tesi Lapcha Pass, and the Dhaulagiri circuit was to be the grand finale of a much longer expedition. It was first explored by Maurice Herzog's famous French expedition of 1950 when they reached the summit of Annapurna, having previously investigated the approaches to Dhaulagiri. (The higher of two passes on the route is still called French Pass.) The trail starts from near Marpha on the Kali Gandaki river and circles the main range to the north, crossing both passes (over seventeen thousand feet) before dropping down into the remote Myagdi valley west of Dhaulagiri. In the event, we were caught by winter snows which arrived a few weeks early. Several days and nights of heavy falls brought the snowline almost down to the villages in the valley, below ten thousand feet, and we knew there was little chance of getting our porters safely over the passes. We hung around for a couple of days, in hope, but finally set off for Pokhara, a week's walk away. When we climbed out of the Kali Gandaki valley three days later and had our last sight of the Dhaulagiri range from the top of the pass at Ghorepani, the snow was still unbroken, low down into the valley.

In 1996 I returned to the Kali Gandaki and Dhaulagiri, with another friend (and fellow-photographer), Iain Roy. This time we were approaching from Pokhara, crossing the little pass at Ghorepani, and before attempting the Dhaulagiri circuit were going to spend some time acclimatising on the high but little-known Thulobugin Lekh (ridge) on the east side of the Gandaki valley. As we reached Ghorepani the view north to the mountains matched exactly my memory of it from all those years before. Even from nearly thirty miles away, you could see how thickly the snow lay, far down on the shoulders of the hills below the route we hoped to attempt. I knew instinctively that, just as back then in 1984, these were the first snows of winter come early, and we were unlikely to get over those passes.

Two or three weeks later, with Thulobugin behind us, and some time spent exploring the upper Kali Gandaki and the medieval villages of southern Mustang, we returned through Marpha and Tukuche on our way back to Pokhara. Several days of heavy rain, falling as snow on the ridges above us, had dispelled any lingering thoughts that a few days' sunshine would clear most of the snow from French Pass, and in fact all the high passes in the region had already been closed for more than a week. Just one group had managed to get through from Beni, to the south-west of the Dhaulagiri group, reversing our intended route. There were nine trekkers, who had with them five experienced Sherpas and eighteen fully-equipped porters. Even so, it had taken them nine days from Dhaulagiri base-camp to Thapa Pass above Tukuche, a distance often covered in three, and they had had to force a way through shoulder-deep snow, with the wind erasing their tracks behind them. I felt a little better when we heard this, as we were unlikely to have got through with our more limited resources. Even had we succeeded, we would have been descending, not into the Kali Gandaki valley with its towns and villages bursting with produce, but into the desolate and uninhabited gorge of the Myagdi Khola.

It is never a good feeling, wondering if you have given up some prize because of excess caution, but I felt justified, almost. When we were back in Kathmandu, waiting for a flight home, a rumour surfaced that another party on the same route had had a European fatality; I never found out whether this was true or not, but it seemed possible. For myself, I am sorry not to have been around Dhaulagiri, and still harbour thoughts of going back.

Sunset light on ice-fall, Tesi Lapcha

Porters haul loads, Drolambo Glacier

Approaching the summit of the pass

Descending from Tesi Lapcha, on the Khumbu side

Jharkot, south Mustang

The Kali Gandaki in autumn, near Larjung

Kagbeni, and the hills of Mustang

Kagbeni gompa (monastery)

Jharkot gompa, Mustang

Tibetan girl, Mustang

Chortens near Jharkot, and Mustang Himal

The Kali Gandaki valley, south of Kagbeni

Muktinath Himal, and the village of Chhinga, Mustang

Monsoon clouds and foothills above Dharan, East Nepal

Newly-planted rice above the Tamur River, East Nepal

Lhonak, Kangchenjunga region

Summit of Wedge Peak, Kangchenjunga range

Jannu from below Lapsang La

Porters approaching the summit of the Lapsang La (pass)

Kabru (left) and Rathong Peak, on the descent from Lapsang La

I discovered that the wind murmering in the leaves and the water roaring in the gorge spoke with voices of their own; alone on the high pastures, strange feelings possessed me, to which I could not give a name.

– Giusto Gervasutti 'Gervasutti's Climbs'

Annapurna, to which we had gone empty-handed, was a treasure on which we should live for the rest of our days. With this realisation, we turn the page.

– Maurice Herzog 'Annapurna'

Jannu, from Kambachen.

THE THULOBUGIN RIDGE

High on the east side of the Kali Gandaki valley, a narrow ridge some eight miles long is suspended mid-way between two giants of the Himalayas - Annapurna and Dhaulagiri. The haunt, in spring and summer, of solitary herdsmen who bring flocks of sheep, cattle and goats up to the high pastures, by late autumn it is deserted. Herzog's expedition, in 1950, found a way up from the village of Chhoya, and crossed the ridge on their way in to establish a base-camp below the north face of Annapurna One; it still sees the occasional passage of climbing expeditions on their way to attempt this now classic route. Apart from these few, there is little traffic on the Thulobugin Ridge.

On my trek in 1996 with Iain Roy, we had decided to use the ridge as a training exercise for harder things we hoped would come later, and as Thulobugin offers unrivalled views of the Annapurna and Dhaulagiri ranges we also expected to take advantage of that, for some photography. We were intending to climb the long southern tail of the ridge and descend by Herzog's 1950 route. Two successive days of hard climbing from the village of Dana saw us camped in a hollow on the ridge at about thirteen thousand feet (4000m), a world away from the busy trail down in the valley. Here our compact little group was alone, and in all the time we spent on Thulobugin we saw only three other human beings, two of those in the far distance. The ridge hangs above the Kali Gandaki like a tightrope, and the views into the valley are aerial - though it is not downwards that the eyes are drawn. Across the impressive gorge of the Miristi Khola, just a mile or two away all the Annapurnas lie strung along the eastern horizon, and westwards huge Dhaulagiri dominates all its surroundings. Tukuche Peak, Mukut Himal and the snow-covered hills of Mustang fade away beyond the furthest reaches of the Kali Gandaki valley, and directly along the ridge Nilgiri fills the northern sky. There is nothing between the onlooker and any of this but clear mountain air, and only to the south where ranks of hazy foothills merge finally into the Indian plain, is there any break in the encircling ring of peaks.

The high Thulobugin area, unsurprisingly, is sacred to the Thakali people of the valley below, whose brand of Buddhism is still mingled with the ancient animistic religions of Nepal, in which all natural objects - mountains, rivers, trees, the sky - were the homes of gods. Where we first came onto the crest of the ridge, a rough, hand-lettered notice decorated with ribbon and sprigs of juniper warned whoever might pass by that they were entering hallowed ground. Above our camp, stone altars still bore signs of rites and offerings, and later as we progressed along the ridge towards the foot of Nilgiri there were many of these altars, singly and in groups, placed at any auspicious point. Concentrated close to Nilgiri there were also hermits' cells - low, roofless structures, with a central hearth, sometimes a small table or altar, and a niche built into the inner gable. Most were in good repair - these were not ruins - but there was little evidence of any recent occupation, and even the hearths showed no trace of charcoal or ash. At times when they were occupied, roofing such as wattle may have been brought up from the valley, and at other points along the ridge we had seen herdsmen's temporary shelters - primitive structures of hooped bamboo over which a woven mat could be thrown. These did bear recent traces of occupation - charcoal in the hearths, beds of dry grass, and even scraps of plastic waste - for these days roofing materials are as likely to be plastic sheeting as the traditional woven reeds or split-cane. At our last camp-site, directly under the huge south face of Nilgiri and a little below the crest of the Thulobugin ridge, we were overlooked by several of the stone cells. From here the Annapurnas were invisible, and if Nilgiri was not found sufficiently impressive, across the dark void of the Kali Gandaki, the squat and massive pyramid of Dhaulagiri was an awe-inspiring presence. Enormous glaciers poured down its flanks between black ridges of appalling length, and from mid-morning each day dark cloud swirled around it, though rarely obscuring the summit from which spindrift streamed, in a plume which could be miles long. That a simple, devout people who revered nature might have wished to come here for worship or contemplation - or to try to placate these terrifying mountain gods - was easy to understand.

On our last day on the ridge the weather, which had been fine, suddenly changed and we woke to cold winds, grey skies and the threat of worse to come. The moderate altitude of fourteen thousand, five hundred feet (4400m) was not high enough to worry us, but it was time to push on and we had no desire to be caught up there in prolonged rain or snow. We headed downhill, with regrets to be leaving so soon and many a backward glance up to the ridge. Down in the valley, in Kalopani two days later, the weather had not improved, and when the cloud lifted to reveal Thulobugin, it was plastered with snow throughout its length.

Stream and undergrowth near Dana, Kali Gan

Corn-store, Dana, Kali Gandaki

Chhoya village and Dhaulagiri

The Kali Gandaki valley, from Thulobugin ridge

Dhaulagiri and Tukuche Peak, from Thulobugin ridge

Sunset light on the Annapurnas, from Thulobugin ridge

How deep our sleep last night in the mountain's heart, beneath the trees and stars, hushed by solemn-sounding waterfalls. And our first pure mountain day, warm, calm, cloudless; how immeasurable it seems, how serenely wild.

– John Muir 'My First Summer in the Sierras'

Twelve miles away across the valley of the Imja Khola stood the Nuptse-Lhotse ridge, with the peak of Everest appearing behind. But even this stupendous wall . . . . seemed dwarfed by the slender spires of fluted ice that towered all about us, near and utterly inaccessible.

– Eric Shipton '1951 Everest Reconnaissance'

Nilgiri South and hermit's cell, Thulobugin

Heart Of The Himalaya

Though I have called Nepal the heart of the Himalaya, perhaps the true centre of all things Himalayan is the region at whose head Everest stands. It is called the Khumbu, the heartland of a people whose name has become inseparable from the very notion of Himalayan climbing - the Sherpas. The wider region is known as Solu Khumbu, and extends from the Tibetan border to the southern reaches of the Dudh Khosi valley, though Khumbu with its famous mountain town, Namche Bazar, is widely regarded as the Sherpas' symbolic home. They are a homogenous group who migrated south from Tibet some centuries ago, and inhabit the high valleys in many parts of central and eastern Nepal, from Helambu just north of Kathmandu all the way east to the valleys below Kangchenjunga.

On my first visit in 1979, like most I was familiar with images of the Everest region, and with its history. I had been in high mountains before, in the Pyrenees, in the French and Swiss Alps, and in Japan; nothing, however, had prepared me for the glories of Khumbu. Those who fly in to the little airstrip perched on the hillside at Lukla may get some inkling from the cabin windows, of what awaits them, but for those who walk from the roadhead at Jiri (or as I did from Lamosangu) surprisingly little can be seen of the big mountains until you are right among them: a far-away view from a dawn ridge or a glimpse down some narrow side-valley, but little more. Around Lukla, the summit of Karyolung just peeps over the western rim of the Dudh Khosi valley, and Kongde Ri is the only mountain which is fully visible. Further north, even these disappear behind steepening valley-walls until only Khumbila, a rocky peak at the head of the valley behind Namche Bazar, can be seen. Halfway up the final slope to Namche there is a brief sighting of the distant Lhotse-Nuptse ridge, with the very tip of Everest just visible.

Namche lies at more than eleven thousand feet (3400m) in a natural amphitheatre high on a hillside above the confluence of the Imja and Nangpo rivers, and in a dramatic situation. Across the Nangpo to the west, the long ridge of Kongde Ri almost fills the entire field of vision, and in the east the razor-sharp peaks of Kangtega and Thamserku are two miles overhead but only four or five miles away; the angle of elevation is quite unreal.

In recent years the sheer number of visitors

has inevitably caused some change of attitude on the part of many of the Sherpa people, who are not now so overtly friendly and open as they once were. When I was first here, anyone seen in company with another Sherpa was treated as an honoured guest and invited indoors for chang, buttered tea and whatever food could be quickly prepared - often hot, spicy potatoes cooked with garlic and chili. The local community is small; in the entire Khumbu region the native population is below three thousand, and everyone knows everyone. Although my great friend Nima Wangchu comes from Kharikhola in the Solu area, he had lived in the village of Kunde, working and studying at the New Zealand medical post there. He was well-known and popular, and as we walked up through Kunde and Khumjung, the invitations came thick and fast. Today, when trekkers pour through by the thousand during the season, the local people cannot possibly open their doors to so many.

The relationship has been changed in other ways, too, by the growth in trekking business. Originally, the Sherpas were a trading people, living too high in the mountains to exist solely on their own meagre agriculture, and acted as middlemen between Tibet on the one hand and southern Nepal, and even India, on the other. The closing of the Tibetan border after the Chinese takeover in 1950 was a bitter blow which abruptly ended most of their trade, and the opening of the mountains to climbing and exploration came in the nick of time. The Sherpas soon found themselves working for expeditions which headed initially to Everest, but soon to many other peaks in and around Khumbu. They were natural mountaineers, superbly adjusted to life at high altitude, and in such a small community, the earnings generated by the expeditions made a huge difference. The Sherpas settled down to a new routine of tending their fields and yaks in the winter and summer, and going on expeditions in spring and autumn. When the expeditions went home, life in the Khumbu soon returned to normal, and because the visiting climbers brought everything they needed with them, and spent their time high in the mountains, there was no need for facilities to be provided for them down in the villages.

In the wake of the expeditions came trekking groups, who certainly did want services and facilities. Some Sherpa villagers began to open their homes to provide accommodation; soon, the first lodges were built, and Khumbu had taken a step on the road to the development of a tourist industry. In 1979, this was still in its infancy, and the people were not nearly as reliant on tourism for their livelihood as they now are; the relationship with visitors was not based so fundamentally on commerce, as it now largely is; and friendship and hospitality were a major part of the interchange.

Lukla, with its dramatic airstrip perched high on the valley-side, was the first place really to develop, and even back then in 1979 it was relatively modern and prosperous. Many more large lodges and hotels were built as clients poured in by air, or by bus and jeep from the new road-head at Jiri - just a few days' walk away - and the local population was soon to become over-dependent on tourism for their livelihood. As a result, they were the first to suffer when large-payload helicopters became available in Kathmandu, and started to fly charters - and before long, regular flights - in and out of the upper Khumbu area, completely bypassing Lukla's hotels and services, which were soon facing bankruptcy. Mass picketing of the helicopter landing areas was one of the methods they used to bring their difficulties to the attention of the authorities in distant Kathmandu. It is a problem which is still not quite solved, but the best solution might be to make people walk again (after all, isn't it why they come to Nepal?) - best for them, best for the locals and certainly best for the Khumbu. The nuisance posed by overcrowding and litter could be brought back under control, and how much better an experience it is anyway - to walk to the mountains.

There is surely no finer place on earth than the upper Khumbu valley, close to where the Khumbu and Changri Glaciers converge below the soaring western face of Nuptse, a diamond summit etched against the blue. Arriving there by your own efforts, having walked from the green humid valleys and steamy jungles of the lowlands, will always be a memorable thing to do. At last you climb above a glacier to stand in a circle of towering ice-peaks, and with every little gain in height fresh wonders are revealed; from each new vantage-point another gleaming summit appears. A powder-snow avalanche avalanche pours silently down the flanks of Nuptse across the valley, shark-fins of ice glint from the glacier, boulders skid beneath your feet and rumble down the moraine - the only sound to disturb the ringing silence. For many, it is the closest thing to a religious experience. You gaze endlessly, as if to etch those glorious summits indelibly on the memory and make them always your own. Everest, Nuptse, Ama Dablam, Kangtega, Thamserku, Taweche, Cholatse, Pumori, Lingtren, Changtse, Everest - the circle is complete.

Eventually you will turn away from them and walk back down the valley to Namche, Lukla and the plane home; but you will never forget.

Porters beside the Khimti Khola, Everest trail

Karantichap, on the Everest trail

Lake and un-named peaks south of Gokyo

Four scenes from Mane Rimdu, Thyangboche

Masked dancer, Mane Rimdu festival, Thyangboche

Ama Lapcha, in the Chukung valley south of Lhotse

Changri Shar glacier, upper Everest valley

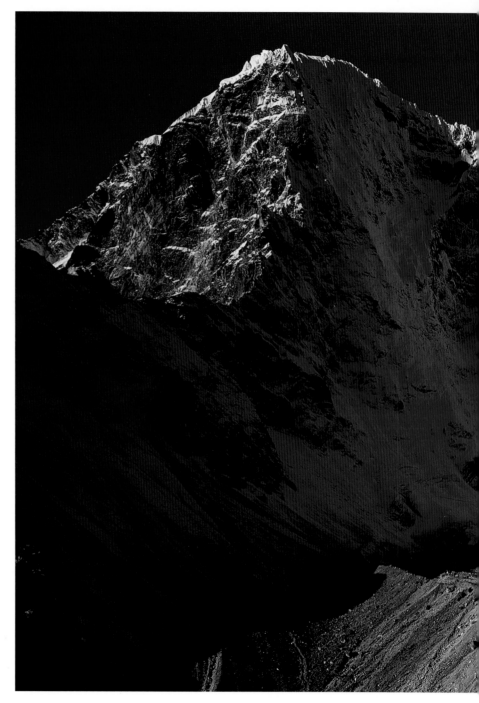

Taweche and Cholatse, Everest region

Taweche and Cholatse, from Gokyo Peak

Un-named peaks above Thame, Khumbu

Early light on Taweche

The summit of Ama Dablam

The Everest group, from Lobuche Peak

The hills beyond Rathong . . . . were divided by pleasant glens, and concealing in their hollows innumerable lakelets, ideal sites for the hotels and pensions of the future.

– Douglas Freshfield 'Round Kangchenjunga'

There was a furore ten years ago about garbage . . . . this was not an important issue compared to the current problems of sanitation, overgrazing, deforestation, landslides and uncontrolled development of hotels for trekkers.

– Stan Armington 'Trekking in Nepal '

Everest and Nuptse, from Kala Patar

THE VIEW FROM POON HILL

A few hundred feet above the village called Ghorepani on the Pokhara-Jomosom trail, there is a famous hill-top from which the entire Dhaulagiri Himal and much of the Annapurna range are gloriously visible. I don't know the etymology of the name Poon Hill, but that of Ghorepani is obvious - it means Horse Water. The trail from Pokhara, down in the southern foothills, runs up to Jomosom and continues north from there via Mustang across low, easy passes into Tibet. It is one of the few footpaths anywhere in Nepal which are not too steep for pack-animals, and for hundreds of years great caravans of horses and mules would come down out of Tibet bearing wool, yak-hides, sheepskins and salt, returning with bales of cloth, and rice and other agricultural products. After the long haul to the top of the pass at Ghorepani, the drivers would stop to water their animals at the stream, and to rest and take some tea themselves.

Mule-trains can still be seen today, though the commodities they carry are very different. The Chinese invasion of Tibet in 1950 put an immediate end to cross-border trade, and Nepal now gets her much-needed salt from India; the south-bound caravans originate no further north than Mustang, and during the season will be carrying mainly potatoes. But the goods which head north have changed, indeed. Since the late 1970's, the old mule-road has been progressively taken over by modern trekking, and is now one of the most heavily-used trails anywhere in the Himalayas. All the way from Pokhara - through the green countryside, up the forested slopes to the ridge at Ghorepani, down again to the Kali Gandaki and up the valley to Jomosom - you can never be more than a mile or two from the local version of a lodge, hotel, cafe or restaurant, and every village positively bristles with their name-boards. The pack-animals now carry tea and teeshirts, coffee, sugar, beer, Coca Cola and Fanta, cigarettes, shampoo, 35mm film and a host of other consumer-goods which western trekkers want, or can be persuaded, to buy. This modern trade has a long ancestry. The shrines of Muktinath at the head of the Kali Gandaki valley, where natural gas seeps through the rocks beside a fresh-water spring, draw pilgrims from all over Nepal and northern India for the holy combination of fire, earth, air and water, set in a cradle of spectacular peaks. The local Thakali people have good commercial instincts, and the provision of services to this passing-trade has always been second nature to them. Though many traditional pilgrims, mainly Hindu, still use the trail, their numbers are insignificant beside the hordes of back-packers who swarm through during spring and autumn, and to whom the signs proclaim 'Mexican Food' 'Vegetarian Lasagne' 'Cold Beer' and more. Here and there among the modern lodges and painted signs for hot showers, heated rooms and foreign food, a traditional Nepali inn sits back from the trail, its rooms given over to the storage of straw and animal-fodder, its elaborately-carved wooden windows and shutters looking down on a courtyard where the only guests will be a few wandering sheep or goats. The transition is complete.

This type of change is not confined to Nepal (nor is it wholly bad) but perhaps the degree of change must soon be questioned. How long will it be before the numbers of foreign tourists passing through regions like these have effectively destroyed the very thing they came to experience; or has it already happened?

It is futile to go to a country like Nepal in search of solitude - the fertile low-country is densely-populated, and to enjoy the mountain wildernesses you must inevitably take your own team with you - either way you cannot be alone. But few tourists, surely, go anywhere in order to meet thousands of their own kind. Of course, the mountains are still there, but there is already too much in the foreground, too many heads to look over (as it were), for the views to be enjoyed. Even in 1984, the Kali Gandaki valley was being called 'the apple-pie trail', and at the very least the atmosphere of many of these places has irrevocably changed, probably not for the better. There is something a little incongruous about walking through some of the highest and finest mountains on earth, in constant company with people, many of whom seem to have come mainly to acquire a good tan, or to score with the opposite sex. It seems that for many young westerners, this has become just another destination to be ticked-off on the list - why should they act any differently in Nepal than in Majorca or Bali (or Brighton)? The answer is long and complex, but perhaps might include the notions that behaviour should always be appropriate to surroundings, and that local people should be treated with a little respect and dignity; the more so when they are essentially simple and unsophisticated.

I first visited the little pass at Ghorepani in 1979, having come over on a side-trek from the Annapurna Sanctuary. We stopped for the night a couple of miles above the village and so I watched my first dawn over Dhaulagiri, not from Poon Hill, but from a slightly higher point on the same ridge. We were the only people around, though later on the way down into Ghorepani we did meet a couple of Australian backpackers, who were scornful of my reliance on Sherpas and porters. I was quite content, however, with the ability it gave me to camp where and when I liked, for as long as I liked, without being dependent on lodges for food and shelter. When we reached the 'village' it consisted of two or three houses and a large tree by a stream. I passed through again in the mid-80's and saw little change, but returning in 1996 I was expecting some development to have taken place. In the event, I was staggered by the way the place had mushroomed.

About ten minutes' walk below the pass on the Pokhara side, there is now a group of buildings - lodge, restaurant, stores - and at the summit a mini-metropolis with a variety of lodges and hotels, plus restaurants, souvenir shops, food-stores, cafes, (a public telephone!), showers, laundry, and camping-grounds. What was a sleepy backwater has become tourist-town.

We stayed one night and early the next day, before continuing on our way north, joined the ritual viewing of sunrise on Dhaulagiri, from Poon Hill. The climb from Ghorepani takes perhaps fifty minutes, and we set off a little after five am, pleased/surprised to see that there were relatively few others moving at that time of the morning. This, as it turned out, was because we were late-comers. At the top of the hill, *hundreds* of people waited for the dawn. There was a wooden grandstand which provided seating for some; a stall dispensed hot tea and drinking-chocolate; people shouted and laughed, and jostled for position; there was horseplay; lovers kissed and cuddled. It was exactly like being at a football match just before kick-off. We hung around to try to get some pictures, and as we departed a quick head-count revealed about a hundred and sixty people still there; many had already left. On the way downhill I was held up on the narrow footpath behind three individuals who were having an animated conversation about British pop music, and later a discussion of where in Ghorepani they might get the best coffee. Here were three people so unaffected by their surroundings - the greatest peaks of western Nepal - that they had already forgotten them. What stuns one onlooker into awed silence means less to the next, it seems, than getting a decent cup of cappuchino.

As we trekked on, other signs and symptoms of volume tourism came thick and fast. However, because the Nepalese people are predominantly good-hearted and friendly, and western visitors are mostly young and open, relations between them are still pretty good. There are increasing tendencies, however, towards boredom on the part of the locals, and towards a belief by the trekkers that they are constantly being ripped-off (this, in an area where a cup of tea costs twelve cents, and a night's lodgings, a dollar). One of the problems of tourism, in any country where the visitors are much richer than the natives, is that a dreadful mutual contempt eventually sets in. This stage hasn't quite been reached in Nepal, though it cannot be far away if the numbers of tourists continue to increase in the present uncontrolled way. The advantages of limiting their numbers may not yet be obvious to the Nepalese, who depend heavily on tourism for both private and national income, but in time benefits for both sides might become evident. There would be less environmental damage and cultural loss for Nepal - less garbage and less grief. The visitor could enjoy the natural wonders of Nepal without constant distraction by, and competition from, too many others like himself. (After all, crowds at famous view-points apart, nobody hates to see a trekker as much as another trekker . . . . .)

I use that word in a general sense - I certainly don't exempt the members of climbing and scientific expeditions from criticism; nor do I exclude myself, of course. (I was upset for a long time after the Poon Hill experience. What haunted me was not the unexpected exposure to mass tourism, but the sure and sudden knowledge *that I was part of it*.)

Home in London, there was a lot to ponder. I will want to return to Nepal again, but now will have to think seriously whether I should. If I do go, should I limit myself to backpacking - has the old-style trek, complete with porters and Sherpa guide, which I enjoy, had its day? Or is it still perhaps the most sympathetic and environmentally-friendly way to trek? Should we all stay on busy, recognised trails, putting up with each other and limiting harm to areas which are already affected? Should treks and expeditions be made to pay the true cost of environmental repairs; and should Nepal bring in a system of quotas for the most popular routes? There are plenty of similar questions for all potential visitors to Nepal.

In many areas, and with help, the local people are already taking great steps to stabilise and regenerate the environment. Many thousands of tourists will continue to visit Nepal each year (and I will probably be among them). If we all go there with a little more awareness of the problem, and willing to be part of the solution, perhaps Nepal can develop to the benefit of all: her native peoples first and foremost. We take a lot; we must find ways to give back, too.

Truck repair at Melemchigaon, Helan

Truckstop at Mugling, on the Kathmandu-Pokhara road

Street scene in Baglung, with Dhaulagiri

Street scene in Jomosom, upper Kali Gandaki

Dawn at Tumlingtar, east Nepal

Terraced fields at Sinam, east Nepal

136

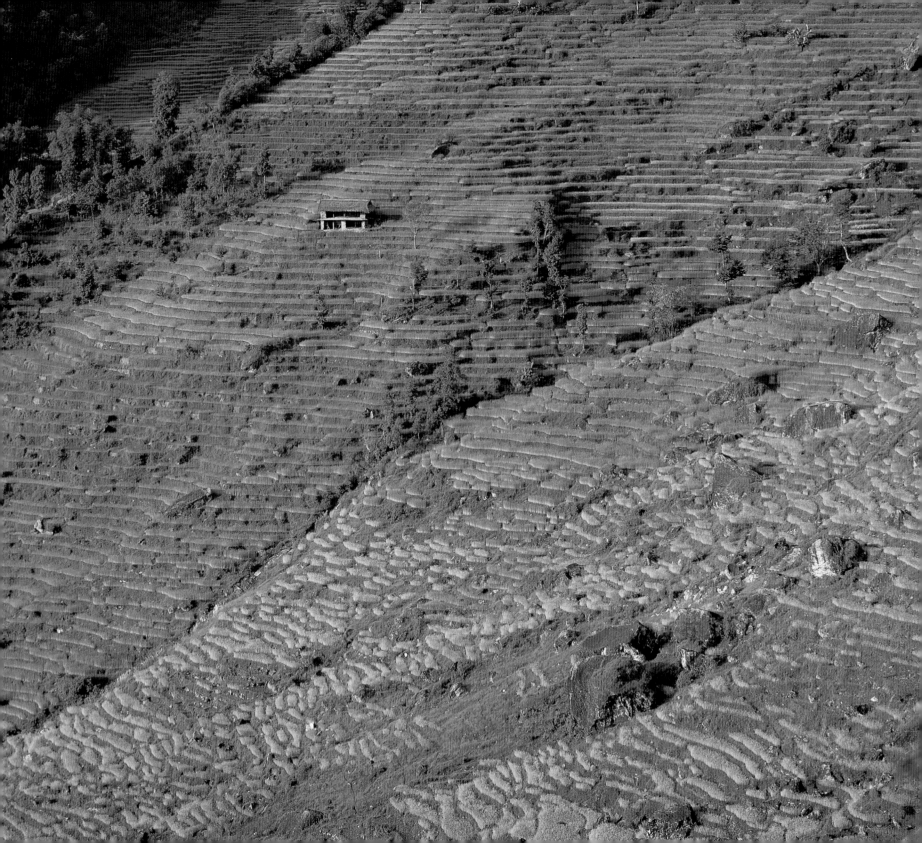

New house at Num, Arun valley, east Nepal

Two women of Sheduwa, Makalu region

Evening ridges above the Arun valley

Early light on the Dhaulagiri range, from Muktinath

Selected Bibliography:

East of Kathmandu, by Tom Weir. Gordon Wright Publishing, 1981.
Everest, by Walter Unsworth. Penguin Books Ltd., 1981.
Abode of Snow, by Kenneth Mason. Diadem Books, 1987.
High Asia, by Jill Neate. Unwin Hyman, 1989.
Nepal, The Kingdom in the Himalayas, by Toni Hagen. Oxford/IBH, 1980.
The Snow Leopard, by Peter Matthiessen. Chatto and Windus, 1979.
The Ascent of Everest, by Sir John Hunt. Hodder & Stoughton, 1954.
Annapurna, by Maurice Herzog. Jonathan Cape, 1952.
Kangchenjunga, the Untrodden Peak, by Charles Evans. Hodder, 1956.
Round Kangchenjunga, by D. Freshfield. (1st publ. 1903) Bibliotheca Himalaya, '79.
The Kangchenjunga Adventure, by Frank Smythe. Camelot Press, 1932.
A Short History of Nepal, by Netra Thapa. Ratna Pustak Bhandar, 1981.
Everest, South-West Face, by Christian Bonington. Hodder & Stoughton, 1982.
Through Tibet to Everest, by Captain JBL Noel. Hodder & Stoughton, 1989.
Annapurna South Face, by Christian Bonington. Penguin Books Ltd., 1973.
Everest The Hard Way, by Christian Bonington, Hodder & Stoughton, 1976.
Sacred Summits, by Peter Boardman. Arrow Books, 1988.
Himalayan Climber, by Doug Scott. Diadem Books, 1992.
All 14 Eight-Thousanders, by Reinhold Messner. Crowood Press, 1987.
The Seven Mountain/Travel Books, by HW Tilman. Diadem, 1985.
The Six Mountain/Travel Books, by Eric Shipton. Diadem, 1985.

Acknowledgements:

The photograph on page 126 is by courtesy of Iain Roy.
My thanks to all my trekking partners - John Beatty who trekked with me in 1981 and 84,
but sadly died in 1993; Mike McQueen who went with me to Ganesh and Langtang in 1987
and Kangchenjunga in 1992; Iain Roy who came to Makalu in 1988 and was snowed in with me
in the Kali Gandaki valley in 1996; to Nima Wangchu Sherpa - a constant companion
on all my treks but one, and to my wife Mayumi and son Sean, who came with me
to Helambu in 1990, and didn't rejoice too obviously at all my other absences.
Last, but far from least, there are the many Sherpas and porters who have helped me,
cheerfully and willingly, during the past eighteen years; and the country people of Nepal
who above all else suffered my curiosity and my camera-lens. Thank you every one.